The
First London
CONFESSION
of FAITH

Of those CHURCHES which
are commonly (though falsely)
called ANABAPTISTS;

Presented to the view of all that fear God, to examine
by the touchstone of the Word of Truth: As likewise
for the taking off those aspersions which are frequently
both in Pulpit and Print, (although unjustly)
cast upon them.

Acts 4:20
We cannot but speak the things which we have seen and heard.

Isaiah 8:20
*To the Law and to the testimony, if they speak not according
to this Rule, it is because there is no light in them.*

II Corinthians 1:9,10
*But we had the sentence of death in ourselves, that we
should not trust in ourselves, but in the living God, which
raiseth the dead; who delivered us from so great a death,
and doth deliver, in whom we trust that he will yet deliver.*

LONDON:
Printed by *Matthew Simons* in *Aldersgate-street.*
1644

Classic Baptist Reprints
2012

To
ALL THAT DESIRE

The lifting up of the Name of the Lord Jesus in sincerity, the poor despised Churches of God in *London* send greeting, with prayers for their farther increase in the knowledge of Christ Jesus.

We question not but that it will seem strange to many men, that such as we are frequently termed to be, lying under that calumny and black brand of Heretics, and sowers of division as we do, should presume to appear so publicly as now we have done: But yet notwithstanding we may well say, to give an answer to such, what David said to his brother, when the Lord's battle was a fighting, I Sam. 29:30. Is there not a cause? Surely, if ever people had cause to speak for the vindication of the truth of Christ in their hands, we have, that being indeed the main wheel at this time that sets us to work; for had anything by men been transacted against our persons only, we could quietly have sitten still, and committed our Cause to him who is a righteous Judge, who will in the great day judge the secrets of all men's hearts by Jesus Christ: But being it is not only us, but the truth professed by us, we cannot, we dare not but speak; it is no strange thing to any observing man, what sad charges are laid, not only by the world, that know not God, but also by those that think themselves much wronged, if they be not looked upon as the chief Worthies of the Church of God, and Watchmen of the City: But it hath fared with us from them, as from the poor Spouse seeking her Beloved, Cant. 5:6,7.
They finding us out of that common road-way themselves walk, have smote us and taken away our veil, that so we may by them be recommended odious in the eyes of all that behold us, and in the hearts of all that think upon us, which they have done both in Pulpit and Print, charging us with holding Free-will, Falling away from grace, denying Original sin, disclaiming of Magistracy, denying to assist them either in persons or purse in any of their lawful Commands, doing acts unseemly in the dispensing the Ordinance of Baptism, not to be named amongst Christians:

All which Charges we disclaim as notoriously untrue, though by reason of these calumnies cast upon us, many that fear God are discouraged and forestalled in harboring a good thought, either of us or what we profess; and many that know not God encouraged, if they can find the place of our meeting, to get together in Clusters to stone us, as looking upon us as a people holding such things, as that we are not worthy to live: We have therefore for the clearing of the truth we profess, that it may be at liberty, though we be in bonds, briefly published a Confession of our Faith, as desiring all that fear God, seriously to consider whether (if they compare what we here say and confess in the presence of the Lord Jesus and his Saints) men have not with their tongues in Pulpit, and pens in Print, both spoken and written things that are contrary to truth; but we know our God in his own time will clear our Cause, and lift his Son to make him the chief cornerstone, though he has been (or now should be) rejected of Master Builders. And because it may be conceived, that what is here published may be but the Judgment of some one particular Congregation, more refined than the rest; We do therefore here subscribe it, some of each body in the name, and by the appointment of seven Congregations, who though we be distinct in respect of our particular bodies, for conveniency sake, being as many as can well meet together in one place, yet all are one in Communion, holding Jesus Christ to be our head and Lord; under whose government we desire alone to walk, in following the Lamb wheresoever he goeth; and we believe the Lord will daily cause truth more to appear in the hearts of his Saints, and make them ashamed of their folly in the Land of their Nativity, that so they may with one shoulder, more study to lift up the Name of the Lord Jesus, and stand for his appointments and Laws; which is the desires and prayers of all the condemned Churches of Christ in London for all Saints.

Subscribed in the Names of seven Churches in London.

William Kiffin.
Thomas Patience.

John Spilsbery.
George Tipping.
Samuel Richardson.

Thomas Skippard.
Thomas Munday.

Thomas Gunne.

John Mabbatt.

John Webb.
Thomas Killcop.

Paul Hobson.
Thomas Goare.

Joseph Phelpes.
Edward Heath.

The
CONFESSION
of FAITH, of those Churches
which are commonly (though falsely)
called ANABAPTISTS.

I. (1)

That God as he is in himself, cannot be comprehended of any but himself, dwelling in that inaccessible light, that no eye can attain unto, whom never man saw, nor can see; that there is but one God, one Christ, one Spirit, one Faith, one Baptism; one Rule of holiness and obedience for all Saints, at all times, in all places to be observed.

I Tim. 6:16; I Tim. 2:5; Eph. 4:4-6; I Cor. 12:4-6,13; John 14; I Tim. 6:3, 13,14; Gal.1:8,9; II Tim. 3:15

II. (2)

That God is of himself, that is, neither from another, nor of another, nor by another, nor for another: But is a Spirit, who as his being is of himself, so he gives being, moving, and preservation to all other things, being in himself eternal, most holy, every way infinite in greatness, wisdom, power, justice, goodness, truth, &c. In this God-head, there is the Father, the Son, and the Spirit; being every one of them one and the same God; and therefore not divided, but distinguished one from another by their several properties; the Father being from himself, the Son of the Father from everlasting, the holy Spirit proceeding from the Father and the Son.

Isa. 44:67; 43:11; 46:9; John 4:24; Ex. 3:14; Rom. 11:36; Acts 17:28; I Cor. 8:6; Pro. 8:22,23; Heb. 1:3; John 1:18; John 15:16; Gal. 4:6

III. (3)

That God hath decreed in himself from everlasting touching all things, effectually to work and dispose them according to the counsel of his own will, to the glory of his Name; in which decree appeareth his wisdom, constancy, truth, and faithfulness;

Wisdom is that whereby he contrives all things; Constancy is that whereby the decree of God remains always immutable; Truth is that whereby he declares that alone which he hath decreed, and though his sayings may seem to sound sometimes another thing, yet the sense of them doth always agree with the decree; Faithfulness is that whereby he effects that he hath decreed, as he hath decreed. And touching his creature man, God hath in Christ before the foundation of the world, according to the good pleasure of his will, foreordained some men to eternal life through Jesus, to the praise and glory of his grace, leaving the rest in their sin to their just condemnation, to the praise of his Justice.

Isa. 46:10; Rom. 11:34-36; Matt. 10:29,30; Eph. 1:11; Col. 2:3; Num. 23:19,20; Jer. 10:10; Rom. 3:4; Isa. 44:10; Eph. 1:3-7; II Tim. 1:9; Acts 13:48; Rom. 8:29,30; Jude ver. 4 & 6; Rom. 9:11-13; Prov. 16:4

IV. (4)

In the beginning God made all things very good, created man after his own Image and likeness, filling him with all perfection of all natural excellency and uprightness, free from all sin. But long he abode not in this honor, but by the subtlety of the Serpent, which Satan used as his instrument, himself with his Angels having sinned before, and not kept their first estate, but left their own habitation; first Eve, then Adam being seduced did wittingly and willingly fall into disobedience and transgression of the Commandment of their great Creator, for the which death came upon all, and reigned over all, so that all since the Fall are conceived in sin, and brought forth in iniquity, and so by nature children of wrath, and servants of sin, subjects of death, and all other calamities due to sin in this world and for ever, being considered in the state of nature, without relation to Christ.

Gen. 1; Col. 1:16; Heb. 11:3; Isa. 45:12; Gen. 1:26; I Cor. 15:45,46; Eccles. 7:31; Ps. 49:20; Gen. 3:1,4,5; II Cor. 11:3; II Peter 2:4; Jude ver. 6; John 8:44; Gen. 3:1,2,6; I Tim. 2:14; Eccles. 7:31; Gal. 3:22; Rom. 5:12,18,19; 6:23; Eph. 2:3; Rom. 5:12

V. (5)

All mankind being thus fallen, and become altogether dead in sins and trespasses, and subject to the eternal wrath of the great God by transgression; yet the elect, which God hath loved with an everlasting love, are redeemed, quickened, and saved, not by themselves, neither by their own works, lest any man should boast himself, but wholly and only by God of his free grace and mercy through Jesus Christ, who of God is made unto us wisdom, righteousness, sanctification and redemption, that as it is written, He that rejoiceth, let him rejoice in the Lord.

Jer. 31:2; Gen. 3:15; Eph. 1:3,7;2:4,9; I Thess. 5:9; Acts 13:38; I Cor. 1:30,31; II Cor. 5:21; Jer. 9:23,24

VI. (6)

This therefore is life eternal, to know the only true God, and whom he hath sent Jesus Christ. And on the contrary, the Lord will render vengeance in flaming fire to them that know not God, and obey not the Gospel of our Lord Jesus Christ.

John 17:3; Heb. 5:9; Jer. 23:5,6; II Thess. 1:8; John 3:36

VII. (7)

The Rule of this Knowledge, Faith, and Obedience, concerning the worship and service of God, and all other Christian duties is not mans inventions, opinions, devices, laws, constitutions, or traditions unwritten whatsoever, but only the word of God contained in the Canonical Scriptures.

John 5:39; II Tim. 3:15-17; Col. 2:18,23; Matt. 15:9

VIII. (8)

In this written Word God hath plainly revealed whatsoever he hath thought needful for us to know, believe, and acknowledge, touching the Nature and Office of Christ, in whom all promises are Yea and Amen to the praise of God.

Acts 3:22,23; Heb. 1:1,2; II Tim. 3:15;-17; II Cor. 1:20

IX. (9)

Touching the Lord Jesus, of whom Moses and the Prophets wrote, and whom the Apostles preached, is the Son of God the Father, the brightness of his glory, the engraven form of his being, God with him and with his holy Spirit, by whom he made the world, by whom he upholds and governs all the works he hath made, who also when the fulness of time was come, was made man of a woman, of the Tribe of Judah, of the seed of Abraham and David, to wit, of Mary that blessed Virgin, by the holy Spirit coming upon her, and the power of the most High overshadowing her, and was also in all things like unto us, sin only excepted.

Gen. 3:15; 22:18; 49:10; Dan. 7:13; 9:24-26; Prov. 8:23; John 1:1-3; Col. 1:1,15-17; Gal. 4:4; Heb. 7:14; Rev. 5:5 with Gen. 49:9,10; Rom. 1:3; 9:5; Matt. 1:16 with Luke 3:23, 26; Heb. 2:16; Isa. 53:3-5; Phil. 2:8

X. (10)

Touching his Office, Jesus Christ only is made the Mediator of the new Covenant, even the everlasting Covenant of grace between God and Man, to be perfectly and fully the Prophet, Priest and King of the Church of God for evermore.

II Tim. 2:15; Heb. 9:15; John 14:6; Heb. 1:2; 3:1; 7:24; Isa. 9:6,7; Acts 5:31

XI. (11)

Unto this Office he was foreordained from everlasting, by the authority of the Father, and in respect of his Manhood, from the womb called and separated, and anointed also most fully and abundantly with all gifts necessary, God having without measure poured the Spirit upon him.

Prov. 8:21; Isa. 42:6; 49:1,5; Isa. 11:2-5; 61:1-3 with Luke 4:17,22; John 1:14,16; 3:34

XII. (12)

In this Call the Scripture holds forth two special things considerable; first, the call to the Office; secondly, the Office itself. First, that none takes this honor but he that is called of God, as was Aaron, so also Christ, it being an action especially of God the Father, whereby a special covenant being made, he ordains his Son to this office: which Covenant is, that Christ should be made a Sacrifice for sin, that he shall see his seed, and prolong his days, and the pleasure of the Lord shall prosper in his hand; which calling therefore contains in itself choosing, foreordaining, sending. Choosing respects the end, foreordaining the means, sending the execution itself, all of mere grace, without any condition foreseen either in men, or in Christ himself.

Heb. 5:4-6; Isa. 53:10; Isa. 42:13; I Peter 1:20; John 3:17; 9:27; 10:36; Isa. 61:1; John 3:16; Rom. 8:32

XIII. (13)

So that this Office to be Mediator, that is, to be Prophet, Priest, and King of the Church of God, is so proper to Christ, as neither in whole, nor in any part thereof, it can be be transferred from him to any other.

I Tim. 2:5; Heb. 7:24; Dan. 5:14; Acts 4:12; Luke 1:33; John 14:6

XIV. (14)

This Office itself to which Christ was called, is threefold, of a Prophet, of Priest, & of a King: this number and order of Offices is showed; first, by mens necessities grievously laboring under ignorance, by reason whereof they stand in infinite necessity of the Prophetical office of Christ to relieve them. Secondly, alienated from God, wherein they stand in need of the Priestly Office to reconcile them: Thirdly, our utter disability to return to him, by which they stand in need of the power of Christ in his Kingly Office to assist and govern them.

Deut. 18:15 with Acts 3:22,23; Ps. 110:3; Heb. 3:1; 4:14,15; 5:6; Ps. 2:6; Acts 26:18; Col. 1:3; 1:21; Eph. 2:12; Cant. 1:13; John 6:44

XV. (15)

Touching the Prophecy of Christ, it is that whereby he hath perfectly revealed the whole will of God out of the bosom of the Father that is needful for his servants to know, believe, and obey; and therefore is called not only a Prophet and a Doctor, and the Apostle of our profession, and the Angel of the Covenant; but also the very wisdom of God, and the treasures of wisdom and understanding.

John 1:18; 12:49,50; 15; 17:8; Deut. 18:15; Matt. 23:10; Heb. 3:1; Mal. 3:1; I Cor. 1:24; Col. 2:3

XVI. (16)

That he might be such a Prophet as thereby to be every way compete, it was necessary that he should be man; for unless he had been God, he could never have perfectly understood the will of god, neither had he been able to reveal it throughout all ages; and unless he had been man, he could not fitly have unfolded it in his own person to man.

John 1:18; 3:13; I Cor. 2:11,16; Acts 3:22 with Deut. 18:15; Heb. 1:1

XVII. (17)

Touching his Priesthood, Christ being consecrated, hath appeared once to put away sin by the offering and sacrifice of himself, and to this end hath fully performed and suffered all those things by which God, through the blood of that his Cross in an acceptable sacrifice, might reconcile his elect only; and having broken down the partition wall, and therewith finished & removed all those Rites, Shadows, and Ceremonies, is now entered within the Veil, into the Holy of Holiest, that is, to the very Heavens, and presence of God, where he for ever liveth and sitteth at the right hand of Majesty, appearing before the face of his Father to make intercession for such as come to the Throne of Grace by the new and living way; and not that only, but makes his people a spiritual House, an holy Priesthood, to offer up spiritual sacrifices acceptable to God through him; neither doth the Father accept, or Christ offer to the Father any other worship or worshippers.

John 17:19; Heb. 5:7-9; 9:26; Rom. 5:19; Eph. 5:12; Col. 1:20; Eph. 2:14-16; Rom. 8:34; I Peter 2:5; John 4:23,24

XVIII. (18)

This Priesthood was not legal, or temporary, but according to the order of Melchizedek; not by a carnal commandment, but by the power of an endless life; not by an order that is weak and lame, but stable and perfect, not for a time, but for ever, admitting no successor, but perpetual and proper to Christ, and of him that ever liveth. Christ himself was the Priest, Sacrifice and Altar: he was Priest, according to both natures, he was sacrifice most properly according to his human nature: whence in the Scripture it is wont to be attributed to his body, to his blood; yet the chief force whereby this sacrifice was made effectual, did depend upon his divine nature, namely, that the Son of God did offer himself for us: he was the Altar properly according to his divine nature, it belonging to the Altar to sanctify that which is offered upon it, and so it ought to be of greater dignity than the Sacrifice itself.

Heb. 7:17-25; 5:6; 10:10; I Peter 1:18,19; Col. 1:20,22; Isa. 53:10; Matt. 20:28; Acts 20:28; Rom. 8:3; Heb. 9:14; 13:10,12,15; Matt. 23:17; John 17:19

XIX. (19)

Touching his Kingdom, Christ being risen from the dead, ascended into heaven, sat on the right hand of God the Father, having all power in heaven and earth, given unto him, he doth spiritually govern his Church, exercising his power over all Angels and Men, good and bad, to the preservation and salvation of the elect, to the overruling and destruction of his enemies, which are Reprobates, communicating and applying the benefits, virtue, and fruit of his Prophecy and Priesthood to his elect, namely, to the subduing and taking away of their sins, to their justification and adoption of Sons, regeneration, sanctification, preservation and strengthening in all their conflicts against Satan, the World, the Flesh, and the temptations of them, continually dwelling in, governing and keeping their hearts in faith and filial fear by his Spirit, which having given it, he never takes away from them, but by it still begets and nourisheth in them faith, repentance, love, joy, hope, and all heavenly light in the soul unto immortality, notwithstanding through our own unbelief, and the temptations of Satan, the sensible sight of this light and love be clouded and overwhelmed for a time. And on the contrary, ruling in the world over his enemies, Satan, and all vessels of wrath, limiting, using, restraining them by his mighty power, as seems good in his divine wisdom & justice to the execution of his determinate counsel, delivering them up to a reprobate mind, to be kept through their own deserts, in darkness and sensuality unto judgment.

I Cor. 15:4; I Peter 3:21,22; Matt. 28:18-20; Luke 24:51; Acts 1:11; 5:30,31; John 19:36; Rom. 14:17; Mark 1:27; Heb. 1:14; John 16:7,15; John 5:26,27; Rom. 5:6-8; 14:17; Gal. 5:22,23; John 1:4,13; 13:1; 10:28,29; 14:16,17; Rom. 11:29; Ps. 51:10,11; Job. 33:29,30; II Cor. 12:7,9; Job chap. 1 & 2; Rom. 1:21; 2:4-6; 9:17,18; Eph. 4:17,18; II Peter chap. 2

XX. (20)

This Kingdom shall be then fully perfected when he shall the second time come in glory to reign amongst his Saints, and to be admired of all them which do believe, when he shall put down all rule and authority under his feet, that the glory of the Father may be full and perfectly manifested in his Son, and the glory of the Father and the Son in all his members.

I Cor. 15:24,28; Heb. 9:28; II Thess. 1:9,10; I Thess. 4:15-17; John 17:21,26

XXI. (21)

That Christ Jesus by his death did bring forth salvation and reconciliation only for the elect, which were those which God the Father gave him; & that the Gospel which is to be preached to all men as the ground of faith, is, that Jesus is the Christ, the Son of the ever-blessed God, filled with the perfection of all heavenly and spiritual excellencies, and that salvation is only and alone to be had through the believing in his Name.

John 15:13; Rom. 8:32-34; 5:11; 3:25; Job 17:2,6,37; Matt. 16:16; Luke 2:26; John 6:9; 7:3; 20:31; I John 5:11

XXII. (22)

That Faith is the gift of God wrought in the hearts of the elect by the Spirit of God, whereby they come to see, know, and believe the truth of the Scriptures, & not only so, but the excellency of them above all other writings and things in the world, as they hold forth the glory of God in his attributes, the excellency of Christ in his nature and offices, and the power of the fulness of the Spirit in its workings and operations; and thereupon are enabled to cast the weight of their souls upon this truth thus believed.

Eph. 2:8; John 6:29; 4:10; Phil. 1:29; Gal. 5:22; John 17:17; Heb. 4:11,12; John 6:63

XXIII. (23)

Those that have this precious faith wrought in them by the Spirit, can never finally nor totally fall away; and though many storms and floods do arise and beat against them, yet they shall never be able to take them off that foundation and rock which by faith they are fastened upon, but shall be kept by the power of God to salvation, where they shall enjoy their purchased possession, they being formerly engraven upon the palms of God's hands.

Matt. 7:24,25; John 13:1; I Peter 1:4-6; Isa. 49:13-16

XXIV. (24)

That faith is ordinarily begot by the preaching of the Gospel, or word of Christ, without respect to any power or capacity in the creature, but it is wholly passive, being dead in sins and trespasses, doth believe, and is converted by no less power, then that which raised Christ from the dead..

Rom. 10:17; I Cor. 1:21; Rom. 9:16; 2:1,2; Ezek. 16:6; Rom. 3:12; 1:16; Eph. 1:19; Col. 2:12

XXV. (25)

That the tenders of the Gospel to the conversion of sinners is absolutely free, no way requiring, as absolutely necessary, any qualifications, preparations, terrors of the Law, or preceding Ministry of the Law, but only and alone the naked soul, as a sinner and ungodly to receive Christ, as crucified, dead, and buried, and risen again, being made a Prince and a Savior for such sinners.

John 3:14,15; 1:12; Isa. 55:1; John 7:37; I Tim. 1:15; Rom. 4:5; 5:8; Acts 5:30,31; 2:36; I Cor. 1:22-24

XXVI. (26)

That the same power that converts to faith in Christ, the same power carries on the soul still through all duties, temptations, conflicts, sufferings, and continually whatever a Christian is, he is by grace, and by a constant renewed operation from God, without which he cannot perform any duty to God, or undergo any temptations from Satan, the world, or men.

I Peter 1:5; II Cor. 12:9; I Cor. 15:10; Phil. 2:12,13; John 15:5; Gal. 19:20

XXVII. (27)

That God the Father, and Son, and Spirit, is one with all believers, in their fulness, in relations, as head and members, as house and inhabitants, as husband and wife, one with him, as light and love, and one with him in his inheritance, and in all his glory; and that all believers by virtue of this union and oneness with God, are the adopted sons of God, and heirs with Christ, co-heirs and joint heirs with him of the inheritance of all the promises of this life, and that which is to come.

I Thess. 1:1; John 14:10,20; 17:21; Col. 2:9,10; 1:19; John 1:17; 20:17; Heb. 2:11; Col. 1:18; Eph. 5:30; 2:22; I Cor. 3:16,17; Isa. 16:5; II Cor. 11:3; Gal. 3:26; John 17:24

XXVIII. (28)

That those which have union with Christ, are justified from all their sins, past, present, and to come, by the blood of Christ; which justification we conceive to be a gracious and free acquittance of a guilty, sinful creature, from all sin by God, through the satisfaction that Christ hath made by his death; and this applied in the manifestation of it through faith.

John 1:7; Heb. 10:14; 9:26; II Cor. 5:19; Rom. 3:23; Acts 13:38,39; Rom. 5:1; 3:25,30

XXIX. (29)

That all believers are a holy and sanctified people, and that sanctification is a spiritual grace of the new Covenant, and effect of the love of God, manifested to the soul, whereby the believer is in truth and reality separated, both in soul and body, from all sin and dead works, through the blood of the everlasting Covenant, whereby he also presseth after a heavenly and Evangelical perfection, in obedience to all the Commands, which Christ as head and King in this new Covenant has prescribed to him.

I Cor. 1:1; I Peter 2:9; Eph. 1:4; I John 4:16; Eph. 4:24; Phil. 3:15; Matt. 28:20

XXX. (30)

All believers through the knowledge of that Justification of life given by the Father, and brought forth by the blood of Christ, have this as their great privilege of that new Covenant, peace with God, and reconciliation, whereby they that were far off, were brought nigh by that blood, and have (as the Scripture speaks) peace passing all understanding, yea, joy in God, through our Lord Jesus Christ, by whom we have received the Atonement.

II Cor. 5:19; Rom. 5:9,10; Isa. 54:10; 26:12; Eph. 2:13,14; Phil. 4:7; Rom. 5:10,11

XXXI. (31)

That all believers in the time of this life, are in a continual warfare, combat, and opposition against sin, self, the world, and the Devil, and liable to all manner of afflictions, tribulations, and persecutions, and so shall continue until Christ comes in his Kingdom, being predestinated and appointed thereunto; and whatsoever the Saints, any of them do possess or enjoy of God in this life, it is only by faith.

Eph. 6:10-13; II Cor. 10:3; Rev. 2:9,10

XXXII. (32)

That the only strength by which the Saints are enabled to encounter with all opposition, and to overcome all afflictions, temptations, persecutions, and trials, is only by Jesus Christ, who is the Captain of their salvation, being made perfect through sufferings, who hath engaged his strength to assist them in all their afflictions, and to uphold them under all their temptations, and to preserve them by his power to his everlasting Kingdom.

John 16:33; Heb. 2:9,10; John 15:5

XXXIII. (33)

That Christ hath here on earth a spiritual Kingdom, which is the Church, which he hath purchased and redeemed to himself, as a peculiar inheritance: which Church, as it is visible to us, is a company of visible Saints called & separarted from the world, by the word and Spirit of God, being baptized into that faith, and joined to the Lord, and each other, by mutual agreement, in the practical enjoyment of the Ordinances, commanded by Christ their head and King.

I Cor. 1:1; Eph. 1:1; Rom. 1:7; Acts 26:18; I Thess. 1:9; II Cor. 6:17; Rev. 18:18; Acts 2:37 with 10:37; Rom. 10:10; Acts 20:21; Matt. 18:19,20; Acts 2:42; I Peter 2:5

XXXIV. (34)

To this Church he hath made his promises, and given the signs of his Covenant, presence, love, blessing, and protection: here are the fountains and springs of his heavenly grace continually flowing forth; thither ought all men to come, of all estates, that acknowledge him to be their Prophet, Priest, and King, to be enrolled amongst his household servants, to be under his heavenly conduct and government, to lead their lives in his walled sheepfold, and watered garden, to have communion here with the Saints, that they may be made to be partakers of their inheritance in the Kingdom of God.

Matt. 28:18-20; II Cor. 6:18; Isa. 8:16; I Tim. 3:15; 4:16; 6:3,5; Acts 2:41,47; Song. 4:12; Gal. 6:10; Eph. 2:19

XXXV. (35)

And all his servants are called thither, to present their bodies and souls, and to bring their gifts God hath given them; so being come, they are here by himself bestowed in their several order, peculiar place, due use, being fitly compact and knit together, according to the effectual working of every part, to the edification of itself in love.

I Cor. 12:6,7,12,18; Rom. 12:4-6; I Peter 4:10; Eph. 4:16; Col. 2:5,6,19; I Cor. 12:12 to the end

XXXVI. (36)

That being thus joined, every Church has power given them from Christ for their better well-being, to choose to themselves meet persons into the office of Pastors, Teachers, Elders, Deacons, being qualified according to the Word, as those which Christ has appointed in his Testament, for the feeding, governing, serving, and building up of his Church, and that none other have power to impose them, either these or any other.

Acts 1:2; 6:3 with 15:22,25; I Cor. 16:3; Rom. 12:7,8; 16:1; I Cor. 12:8,28; I Tim. chap. 3; Heb. 13:7; I Peter 5:1-3

XXXVII. (37)

That the Ministers aforesaid, lawfully called by the Church, where they are to administer, ought to continue their calling, according to God's Ordinance, and carefully to feed the flock of Christ committed to them, not for filthy lucre, but of a ready mind.

Heb. 5:4; Acts 4:32; I Tim. 4:14; John 10:3,4; Acts 20:28; Rom. 12:7,8; Heb. 13:7,17

XXXVIII. (38)

That the due maintenance of the Officers aforesaid, should be the free and voluntary communication of the Church, that according to Christ's Ordinance, they that preach the Gospel, should live on the Gospel and not by constraint to be compelled from the people by a forced Law.

I Cor. 9:7,14; Gal. 6:6; I Thess. 5:13; I Tim. 5:17,18; Phil. 4:15,16

XXXIX. (39)

That Baptism is an Ordinance of the new Testament, given by Christ, to be dispensed only upon persons professing faith, or that are Disciples, or taught, who upon a profession of faith, ought to be baptized.

Matt. 28:18,19; Mark 16:16; Acts 2:37,38; 8:36-38;18:8

XL. (40)

The way and manner of the dispensing of this Ordinance the Scripture holds out to be dipping or plunging the whole body under water: it being a sign, must answer the thing signified, which are these: first, the washing the whole soul in the blood of Christ: Secondly, that interest the Saints have in the death, burial, and resurrection; thirdly, together with a confirmation of our faith, that as certainly as the body is buried under water, and riseth again, so certainly shall the bodies of the Saints be raised by the power of Christ, in the day of the resurrection, to reign with Christ.

The word *Baptizo*, signifying to dip under water, yet so as with convenient garments both upon the administrator and subject, with all modesty. Matt. 3:16; John 3:23; Acts 8:38; Rev. 1:5; 7:14 with Heb. 10:22; Rom. 6:3-6; I Cor. 15:28,29

XLI. (41)

The persons designed by Christ, to dispense this Ordinance, the Scriptures hold forth to be a preaching Disciple, it being no where tied to a particular Church, Officer, or person extraordinarily sent, the Commission enjoining the administration, being given to them under no other consideration, but as considered Disciples.

Isa. 8:16; Matt. 28:16-19; John 4:1,2; Acts 20:7; Matt. 26:26

XLII. (42)

Christ has likewise given power to his whole Church to receive in and cast out, by way of Excommunication, any member; and this power is given to every particular Congregation, and not one particular person, either member or Officer, but the whole.

Acts 2:47; Rom. 16:2; Matt. 18:17; I Cor. 5:4; II Cor. 2:6-8

XLIII. (43)

And every particular member of each Church, how excellent, great, or learned soever, ought to be subject to this censure and judgment of Christ; and the Church ought with great care and tenderness, with due advice to proceed against her members.

Matt. 18:16-18; Acts 11:2,3; I Tim. 5:19-21

XLIV. (44)

And as Christ for the keeping of this Church in holy and orderly Communion, placeth some special men over the Church, who by their office are to govern, oversee, visit, watch; so likewise for the better keeping thereof in all places, by the members, he hath given authority, and laid duty upon all, to watch over one another.

Acts 20:27,28; Heb. 13:17,24; Matt. 24:25; I Thess. 5:14; Mark 13:34,37; Gal. 6:1; I Thess. 5:11; Jude ver. 3,20; Heb. 10:34,35; 12:15

XLV. (45)

That also such to whom God hath given gifts, being tried in the Church, may and ought by the appointment of the Congregation, to prophecy, according to the proportion of faith, and so teach publicly the Word of God, for the edification, exhortation, and comfort of the Church.

I Cor. Chap. 14; Rom. 12:6; I Peter 4:10,11; I Cor. 12:7; I Thess. 5:17-19

XLVI. (46)

Thus being rightly gathered, established, and still proceeding in Christian communion, and obedience of the Gospel of Christ, none ought to separate for faults and corruptions, which may, and as long as the Church consists of men subject to failings, will fall out and arise amongst them, even in true constituted Churches, until they have in due order sought redress thereof.

Rev. chapt. 2 & 3; Acts 15:12; I Cor. 1:10; Eph. 2:16; 3:15,16; Heb. 10:25; Jude ver. 15; Matt. 18:17; I Cor. 5:4,5

XLVII. (47)

And although the particular Congregations be distinct and several Bodies, every one a compact and knit City in itself; yet are they all to walk by one and the same Rule, and by all means convenient to have the counsel and help one of another in all needful affairs of the Church, as members of one body in the comon faith under Christ their only head.

I Cor. 4:17; 14:33,36; 16:1; Matt. 28:20; I Tim. 3:15; 6:13,14; Rev. 22:18,19; Col. 2:6,19; 4:16

XLVIII. (48)

That a civil Magistracy is an ordinance of God set up by God for the punishment of evil doers, and for the praise of them that do well; and that in all lawful things commanded by them, subjection ought to be given by us in the Lord: and that we are to make supplication and prayer for Kings, and all that are in authority, that under them we may live a peaceable and quiet lief in all godliness and honesty.

Rom. 13:1-4; I Peter 2:13,14; I Tim. 2:2

XLIX. (49)

The supreme Magistracy of this Kingdom we believe to be the King and parliament freely chosen by the Kingdom, and that in all those civil Laws which have been acted by them, or for the present is or shall be ordained, we are bound to yield subjection and obedience unto in the Lord, as conceiving ourselves bound to defend both the persons of those thus chosen, and all civil Laws made by them, with our persons, liberties, and estates, with all that is called ours, although we should suffer never so much from them in not actively submitting to some Ecclesiastical Laws, which might be conceived by them to be their duties to establish which we for the present could not see, nor our consciences could submit unto; yet are we bound to yield our persons to their pleasures.

L. (50)

And if God should provide such a mercy for us, as to incline the Magistrates hearts so far to tender our consciences, as that we might be protected by them from wrong, injury, oppression and molestation, which long we formerly have groaned under by the tyranny and oppression of the Prelatical Hierarchy, which God through mercy hath made this present King and parliament wonderful honorable, as an instrument in his hand, to throw down; and we thereby have had some breathing time, we shall, we hope, look at it as a mercy beyond our expectation, and conceive ourselves further engaged for ever to bless God for it.

I Tim. 1:2-4; Ps. 126:1; Acts 9:31

LI. (51)

But if God withhold the Magistrates allowance and furtherance herein; yet we must not withstanding proceed together in Christian communion, not daring to give place to suspend our practice, but to walk in obedience to Christ in our profession and holding forth this faith before mentioned, even in the midst of all trials and afflictions, not accounting our goods, lands, wives, children, fathers, mothers, brethren, sisters, yea, and our own lives dear unto us, so we many finish our course with joy: remembering always we ought to obey God rather then men, and grounding upon the commandment, commission and promise of our Lord and master Jesus Christ, who as he hath all power in heaven and earth, so also hath promised, if we keep his commandments which he hath given us to the end of the world: and when we have finished our course, and kept the faith, to give us the crown of righteousness, which is laid up for all that love his appearing, and to whom we must give an account of all our actions, no man being able to discharge us of the same.

Acts 2:40,411 4:19; 5:28-29,41; 20:23; I Thess. 3:3; Phil. 1:27-29; Dan. 3:16,17; 6:7,10,22,23; Matt. 28:18-20; I Tim. 6:13-15; Rom. 12:1,2; I Cor. 14:37; II Tim. 4:7,8; Rev. 2:10; Gal. 2:4,5

LII. (52)

And likewise unto all men is to be given whatsoever is their due; tributes, customs, and all such lawful duties, ought willingly to be by us paid and performed, our lands, goods, and bodies, to submit to the Magistrate in the Lord, and the Magistrate every way to be acknowledged, reverenced, and obeyed, according to godliness; not because of wrath only but for conscience sake. And finally, all men so to be esteemed and regarded, as is due and meet for their place, age, estate and condition.

Rom. 13:5-7; Matt. 22:21; Titus 3; I Peter 2:13; Eph. 5:21,22; 6:1,9; I Peter 5:5

LII [sic]. (52)

And thus we desire to give unto God that which is God's, and unto Caesar that which is Caesar's, and unto all men that which belongeth unto them, endeavoring ourselves to have always a clear conscience void of offense towards God, and towards man. And if any take this that we have said, to be heresy, then do we with the Apostle freely confess, that after the way which they call heresy, worship we the God of our Fathers, believing all things which are written in the Law and in the Prophets and Apostles, desiring from our souls to disclaim all heresies and opinions which are not after Christ, and to be steadfast, unmovable, always abounding in the work of the Lord, as knowing our labor shall not be in vain in the Lord.

Matt. 22:21; Acts 24:14-16; John 5:28; II Cor. 4:17; I Tim. 6:1-5; I Cor. 15:58,59

I Cor. 1:24
Not that we have dominion over your faith, but are helpers of your joy: for by faith we stand.

Notes:

Made in the USA
Middletown, DE
24 January 2025

69957028R00015